T0121013

# GALATIANS
## A COMMENTARY

MARC D. SIMON

**author**HOUSE®

*AuthorHouse™*
*1663 Liberty Drive*
*Bloomington, IN 47403*
*www.authorhouse.com*
*Phone: 833-262-8899*

*Published by AuthorHouse  12/29/2022*

*ISBN: 978-1-6655-7927-8 (sc)*
*ISBN: 978-1-6655-7928-5 (e)*

# Contents

# Introduction

NEXT TO ROMANS, NO OTHER WRITING has impacted the shape of reformed theology and teaching more than Paul's letter to the Galatians. So important was it that Martin Luther affectionately referred to the letter as his Katie von Bora – *which was the name of his wife*, stating that in some ways he was married to the letter as well.

Like Romans, Galatians is rooted in Paul's conviction that through the resurrection of Jesus, God's new creation has burst in upon the old with redeeming power and vindication for all those made part of Christ's body by faith.

Unlike Romans though, Galatians isn't primarily an exposition on the gospel itself or how we get saved. Though faith and works factor heavily in the letter, sin itself is rarely mentioned, salvation not at all, and the resurrection only once.

What is really at issue in Galatians is the inclusion of all people in the single, multi-ethnic family of God… on earth…right here…right now. Who is in and who is out? Who belongs? And on what basis? These are the real issues being debated by the churches to whom Paul is writing.

## Who were the Galatians?

While there is still debate on the exact identity of Paul's intended audience, his letter was likely addressed to churches in the Roman province of Southern Galatia. This region includes Pisidian Antioch, Iconium, Lystra and Derbe; which are specifically named as places where Paul established churches on his first missionary journey (cf. Acts 13-14).

This means that Galatians probably has an earlier dating than some have suggested and was likely written in the time between Paul's first mission in Southern Galatia and the Jerusalem Council in Acts 15, where many of the issues at play seem to have been addressed.

## The Occasion and Purpose of the Letter

Paul's converts in Galatia were mostly non-Jews who embraced his teaching about Jesus, were baptized (3:26-28) and experienced the work of the Holy Spirit among them (cf. 3:2- 5, 4:6).

Though his readers were running what he calls "a good race" (5:7), other teachers had come among them after Paul's departure, preaching "a different gospel" (1:6) and insisting that Jewish Law was binding on all members of the church. These teachers also argued that Paul himself was a second-rate apostle with no real authority.

The identity of Paul's opponents is never stated outright in the letter, but we should not suppose that the conflict was about Jewish and anti-Jewish sentiment. Paul himself was (1) a Jew, (2) a follower of Christ, and (3) an apostle.[1] The conflict wasn't about being "Jewish" or "Christian," but about Paul and his opponents having different Jewish-Christian interpretations of the gospel and its spread among Gentiles.

It is the spiritual identity of the new churches in the Mediterranean that Paul and his opponents are vying for. Were these churches to see themselves as part of the community of Judaism, or as part of a new and distinctive community altogether, something neither completely Jewish nor pagan, but Christian instead?

Paul's answer is that new believers were now part of the community of the Messiah by faith alone and not works of the Law. Followers of Jesus, no matter what their ethnic or moral background, were incorporated into the family of God by the grace and action of God alone, and not by outward marks of Jewish identity, Sabbath keeping, or other works of the Law.

---

[1] Despite his mission to the Gentiles, Paul never ceased to identify himself as a racial or ethnic Jew, *e.g.*, *"I am a Jew" (Acts 22:3)*, *"I too am an Israelite" (Romans 11:1)*, *"a Hebrew of Hebrews" (Phil. 3:5)*.

COMMENTARY ON PAUL'S LETTER TO THE
# GALATIANS

# I. No Other Gospel

## Galatians 1:1–17

1 Paul, an apostle – though not from men nor through the agency of a man, but through Jesus Christ and God the Father, who raised him from the dead – ² and all the brothers who are with me.

To the churches of Galatia:

³ Grace and peace to you from God our Father and Jesus Christ, our Lord, ⁴ who gave himself for our sins that he might deliver us from the present evil age, by the will of our God and Father, ⁵ to whom be glory forever. Amen.

⁶ I marvel that you are so quickly turned from the one who called you into the grace of Christ to a different gospel, ⁷ which is not really a gospel at all. But some are troubling you and trying to pervert the gospel of Christ. ⁸ But if we, or even an angel from heaven, proclaim a different gospel than the one we have already preached, then let such a one be cast out! ⁹ As we've already said, I say again: if anyone preaches a gospel different from the one you received, let him be cast out!

¹⁰ Am I now seeking the approval of men or God? Is it man I'm trying to please? If I were still pleasing man, I would not be the servant of Christ.

¹¹ For I'm telling you, brothers, the gospel I preached was not according to man. ¹² I neither received it from man, nor was I taught it by others, but through revelation of Jesus Christ.

¹³ For you have heard of my previous life in Judaism. And how I persecuted the church of God and ravaged it. ¹⁴ And was advancing beyond many of my own age and people, being more zealous for the traditions of my fathers. ¹⁵ But when it pleased God – who set me apart from my mother's womb and called me by his grace – ¹⁶ to reveal his Son in me that I might preach him among the nations, I did not immediately commit myself to men, ¹⁷ nor confer with those in Jerusalem who were apostles before me; but went away into Arabia, and then returned to Damascus.

---

## 1. Paul, an apostle – though not from men nor through the agency of a man, but through Jesus Christ and God the Father.

Paul begins his letter by asserting his authority as an "apostle" ("a sent one"), emphasizing that the source of his apostolic calling was neither a man nor a human institution, but God himself.

Though he can elsewhere speak of "receiving" and "passing on" traditions related to the gospel (e.g., 1 Cor. 11:23-25, 15:3-7), he is adamant that his commission as an apostle was independent of such processes, and a result of his own personal encounter with the risen Jesus, who says of the apostle Paul:

> He is a chosen instrument of Mine to bear My name before the Gentiles and kings and the sons of Israel. (Acts 9:15, NASB)

**Who raised him from the dead**

So pressing are the matters that prompted Paul's writing, that this is the only explicit reference he makes to the resurrection in the entire letter.

**2. To the churches of Galatia.**

A distinctive of Paul's letters is that they are each addressed to churches in a specific city (e.g., "to all in Rome," "to the church in Corinth," "to the church of the Thessalonians," etc.[2]). Galatians alone is addressed to a plurality of churches in a wider province or region and was likely circulated and read among different assemblies in the area. This would also explain the peculiar absence of any individual greetings or personal names in the letter.

**3. Grace and peace to you from God our Father and Jesus Christ, our Lord.**

The words *grace* and *peace* combine Greek and Hebrew greetings in a way that highlights both the reconciling power (grace) of God and the well-being (peace) of those who receive it by faith.

**4. Who gave himself for our sins.**

It was not a new philosophy or religion that Paul was commissioned to announce, but a Person – *Jesus Christ, our Lord, who gave himself for our sins.* The gospel

---

[2] Philemon is addressed to 3 individuals and the church that gathers in their home.

announced by Paul was about the faithfulness of Jesus the Messiah in dying for our sins.

**That he might deliver us from the present evil age.**

For first century Jews, the history of the world was divided into 2 ages or dispensations: the present age (olam hazeh) of corruption, and the coming age (olam ha-ba) of God's redeeming justice.

> See, I will create new heavens and a new earth. The former things will not be remembered, nor come to mind. But be gladdened and rejoice forever in the new creation I will bring about, for I will create Jerusalem as a delight and its people a joy. (Isa. 65:17-18)

For Paul, the death of Jesus didn't simply procure the forgiveness of our sins; but transposed us into an entirely new reality – *new creation*. It did this by liberating us from the powers at work in "the present age," i.e., *ha olam hazeh.*

> Therefore, if anyone is in Christ, the new creation has come: The old has gone, the new is here! (2 Cor. 5:17, NIV)

**By the will of our God and Father.**

The self-giving action of Jesus in dying for our sins was in accordance with God's will from the beginning, as Christ himself declares on the eve of the crucifixion – *"Yet not my will, but yours be done" (Lk. 22:42).*

Throughout his letter Paul will repeatedly stress to his readers that God was already their "Father." For this reason, they did not have to undergo circumcision or any other works to become children of God or members of the Abrahamic family.

> Because you are now his sons, God has sent the Spirit of his Son into our hearts, crying *Abba, Father*. So, you are no longer a slave, but God's child; and since you are his child, God has also made you an heir. (Gal. 4:6-7)

## 6. I marvel that you are so quickly turned from the one who called you into the grace of Christ...

The one who had truly called the Galatians was neither Paul, nor the other teachers with whom he was in dispute, but God! In turning from the word of grace Paul says they had effectually turned from the grace-giver as well, cf. "from God, who called you" (NLT), "from God, who chose you with his gift" (CEV).

Elsewhere in Galatians (e.g., 1:15, 5:8), as well as Paul's other writings, God is consistently presented as the one who "calls" us. Paul uses the Greek verb *kaléō* (to call, summon, invite) to describe God's gracious act of calling human beings into covenant relationship (e.g., Rom. 8:30, 9:11-12, 1 Cor. 1:9, 1 Thess. 2:12, 5:24).

> I urge you to walk in a manner worthy of the calling you were called to. (Eph. 4:1)

## A different gospel.

The rival Missionaries in Galatia were not urging Paul's Galatian converts to renounce their Christian faith.

Rather, they were preaching a version of the gospel that made observing the Mosaic Law a requirement for those seeking inclusion in the family of God.

## 7. Which is not really a gospel at all.

If the gospel is the triumphant proclamation that Jesus died for our sins and then rose, then any "gospel" that fails to account for the world-transforming effects of his death and resurrection is a "non-gospel."

For the Galatians to have Christ and the Spirit, and then come under Jewish Law was a reversion back into the "present evil age" from which Christ had already redeemed them. Any "gospel" that sanctioned or validated this reversion had to be rejected out of hand as a false gospel.

## 8. Let him be cast out!

Paul here pronounces a curse on anyone perverting the gospel: "Let them be cast out (anathema, "accursed")." The term denotes something laid up, delivered, or given over to God for judgment or destruction.

We should be mindful that Paul is not pronouncing this curse on unbelievers outside of the church, but warning against the heresy of preachers *within the church* who replace the singular gospel of Jesus Christ with a non-gospel, i.e., counterfeit teachings dressed up in the language of Christian faith.

## 10. Is it man that I'm trying to please?

Paul twice uses the phrase: *anthrōpois* (human being) *areskein* (to please or satisfy). His opponents had accused him of being a people-pleaser, i.e., offering non-Jews a watered-down version of the gospel by doing away with the inconvenient requirements of circumcision and Law.

## 11-12. The gospel I preached was not according to man.

Paul is going to argue throughout the letter's opening chapters that his gospel is of divine origin, and his apostleship independent of men. The message he proclaimed in Galatia had been given to him by God, and not the earlier apostles or teachers in Jerusalem.

In v. 11 he uses a somewhat difficult expression in Greek: *to euangelion to euangelisthen hup emou,* literally "the gospel that was gospeled by me." What he is suggesting, though his phrasing is difficult to translate, is that he himself was both a product of the gospel (he had been "gospelized") and its instrument, rather than an independent agent charged with developing its content.

## I neither received it…nor was I taught it…but through revelation of Jesus Christ.

While the Jewish leaders of Paul's time emphasized the authoritative process of transmitting tradition from teacher to student, Paul claimed unmediated access to God's revelation for himself. What he received had not come to him through human tradition or teachers, but "through revelation of Jesus Christ."

But what does this phrase mean? Firstly, the clause is elliptical, lacking a verb. Most translations add "I received it"[3] (NIV, NLT, ESV), since this is the verb Paul begins the verse with, i.e., *"I neither received it... nor was I taught..."*

Secondly, the word revelation (apokalupsis) itself denotes God's activity – *not mans*. It is an act of disclosure from the divine side that reorients perception and knowledge on the human side.

But was Jesus the one who gave revelation to Paul, or was he the one revealed by it? A partial answer can be drawn from vv. 15-16, where Paul states that it pleased God "to reveal his Son." In other words, Paul had received a revelation of Jesus (the Son) from God (the Father).

### 13. For you have heard of my previous life in Judaism.

Paul's retelling of his personal story gives emphasis to two points: [1] the divine origin of his call, and [2] his independence as an apostle from the Jerusalem church and its leaders.

He begins by referencing his earlier life in "Judaism" (Ioudaismos), which designates Jewish life and culture as a whole and not simply the beliefs or doctrines of the Jewish faith.[4] In other words, the term Judaism isn't being used by Paul as a synonym for Jewish religion or beliefs, but for Jewish life itself.

---

[3] *cf.* NIV, NLT, ESV, NASB, AMP, NRSV
[4] Dunn, J.D., *The Epistle To The Galatians* (1993)

## 14. And was advancing beyond many of my own age and people.

The verb "advancing" (proekopton) was widely used by Stoics and other philosophers of Paul's time to describe their progress in the disciplines of wise living. Paul portrays the Judaism of his day as a kind of moral culture in which one could seek to excel or advance in similar fashion.

## Zealous for the traditions of my fathers.

By the Second Temple period the term "zeal" had acquired special meaning within Judaism. Simply put, zeal related to one's efforts to preserve the ethnic and cultural purity of the Jewish people and religion – by violence if necessary.[5]

The most popular model of zeal in the Old Testament was Phinehas, an Israelite who averted a plague from Israel by killing an Israelite dissident and his Midianite lover with a spear (Num. 25:6-9). An act which God rewarded with a unique covenant relation with Phinehas.

> Then the LORD said to Moses, "Phinehas son of Eleazar, son of Aaron the priest, has turned My anger from Israel by being *zealous* for My honor among them, so that I did not consume Israel in My *zeal*. Therefore, tell him that I am making My covenant of peace with him…*because he was zealous for his God,* and made atonement for Israel." (Num. 25:10-13)

---

[5] Hengel, M., *The Zealots: Investigations into the Jewish Freedom Movement* (1961)

Other exemplars of zeal in the Jewish tradition include Mattathias Maccabeus, who initiated the Maccabean rebellion by killing a fellow Israelite for attempting to offer pagan sacrifices in the Temple.

> For he burned with *zeal* for the Law, even as Phinehas did against Zimri son of Salu. (1 Macc. 2:26)

Elijah the prophet is also an exemplar of zeal, and a model with whom Paul draws numerous parallels. After killing the prophets of Baal with the sword (1 Kgs. 18:40) Elijah speaks of his great *zeal* for the LORD, "I have been very *zealous* for the LORD, the God of hosts" (1 Kgs. 19:10).

As a Pharisee it was Paul's zeal for the Law that led him to violently persecute "the church of God" and attempt to destroy it, cf. *"as for zeal, persecuting the church"* (Phil. 3:6).

> But Saul was attempting to destroy the church. Entering their houses, he dragged both men and women to prison. (Acts 8:3)

**15–16. But when it pleased God – who set me apart from my mother's womb and called me by his grace – to reveal his Son in me that I might preach him among the nations...**

While most commentators agree that Paul is referring to his calling on the Damascus Road (cf. Acts 9:1-19, 22:1-21 and 26:2-23), we should avoid superimposing Luke's narrative from Acts on top of Paul's testimony in Galatians.

Firstly, Paul never mentions being on the road to Damascus in his letter. Nor does he speak of the blinding light or voice from heaven. Not because they didn't happen, but because they weren't relevant to his letter.

Instead, he describes his call using language and imagery drawn from Isaiah and Jeremiah, suggesting that his calling was to be understood on the same pattern as God's calling of the prophets in the Old Testament. The writings which Paul echoes prefigure his own election from the womb and ministry of proclamation to the Gentile Nations.

> Before I formed you in the womb I knew you, and before you were born, I set you apart and appointed you as a prophet to the Nations ("to the Gentiles"). (Jer. 1:4-5)

> Listen to me, O coastlands and distant nations. Before I was born the LORD called me; from my mother's womb he spoke my name. (Isa. 49:1)

> It is a light thing that my servant should raise up the tribes of Jacob and people of Israel: I will also give you as a light to the Nations ("to the Gentiles"), that my salvation may reach to the ends of the earth. (Isa. 49:6)

**To reveal his Son in me.**

There are two possible interpretations of the phrase, "to reveal his Son in me." One emphasizing Paul's *reception* of God's revelation and the other emphasizing his *proclamation* of it. Both are valid! God's purpose was not only to reveal his Son *to* Paul, but to reveal him to the Nations *in* and *through* Paul as well.[6]

## 17. But went away into Arabia, and then returned again to Damascus.

Why did Paul go to Arabia, and what did he do while he was there? The best that we can do is speculate on this point. One proposal builds on the fact that Paul's only other mention of Arabia (Gal. 4:25) identifies it as the site of Sinai, where Moses received the Torah.[7]

Like the prophet Elijah, an earlier model of Jewish zeal, Paul may have traveled to Sinai in Arabia to seek God for himself, and to sure up his apostolic calling, much as Elijah did at Sinai ["Horeb the mountain of God"] years before (1 Kgs. 19:7-8). Again, we don't know for sure.

However, Paul ends his time in Arabia by returning to Damascus, just as Elijah had ended his time there before him by returning to Damascus as well.

> The LORD said to him, Go back the way you came, and return to the desert of Damascus. (1 Kgs. 19:15)

---

[6] Hays, *Galatians* (2000), p. 215

[7] Torah (תּוֹרָה) is a Hebrew word meaning "Instruction," "Teaching," or "Law," and is usually used as a referent for the first five books of the Bible. Torah is also used in Jewish tradition as a synonym for the entire Hebrew canon of Scripture, i.e., the TaNaKh (TaNaKh = Torah [Law], Nevi'im [Prophets], and Ketuvim [Writings]).

# II. Jerusalem, Syria, and Antioch

## Galatians 1:18–2:10

[18] Only after three years did I go up to Jerusalem to confer with Cephas and stayed with him fifteen days. [19] I saw none of the other apostles during this time however, except for James, the Lord's brother. [20] I assure you before God that what I'm writing is no lie.

[21] From there I went into Syria and Cilicia [22] where I was personally unknown to the churches of Christ in Judea. [23] They were hearing however, that the one who had once persecuted them was now preaching the faith he had tried to destroy. [24] And they glorified God in me.

**2** Then after fourteen years, I went up to Jerusalem again, only this time with Barnabas and Titus. [2] I went in response to revelation and set before them the gospel I preach among the Gentiles – though privately with those esteemed – lest I be found running or to have run in vain.

[3] But not even Titus, who was with me, was compelled to be circumcised, even though he was a Greek. [4] This only became an issue because of false brothers who came in among us, scrutinizing the freedom we have in Christ, and trying to bring us back into bondage. [5] But we did not yield to them for even an hour, that the truth of the gospel might remain with you.

[6] As for those who were esteemed – and what they were made no difference to me, for God is no respecter of persons – they added nothing to me, [7] but recognized that I had been entrusted with the gospel to the uncircumcised, just as Peter

had been to the circumcision. ⁸ For the One who worked in Peter as an apostle among the circumcised, was now working in me also among the nations. ⁹And James, Cephas and John – who were esteemed as pillars – when they saw the grace that had been given to me, extended to Barnabas and I the right hand of fellowship, agreeing that we should work among the Gentiles, and they among the circumcised. ¹⁰ All they asked was that we remember the poor, the very thing I had already determined to do.

---

## 18. Only after three years did I go up to Jerusalem to confer with Cephas and stayed with him fifteen days.

"Only after three years" likely refers to the time that had passed after Paul's initial calling by God rather than after his time in Arabia.

What Paul is really emphasizing to his readers is how little time he had spent with Peter [Cephas, cf. Jn. 1:42] and the earlier apostles in the past. While he doesn't tell us the specifics of his conversations in Jerusalem, he wants his readers to know that he did not go there to receive instruction in the specifics of the gospel or the traditions about Jesus, for which the earlier apostles would have been the authoritative sources.[8]

---

[8] Paul hardly ever mentions the earlier traditions about Jesus in his writings. His few direct references may be found in 1 Cor. 11:23-26, and perhaps 1 Thess. 4:15-17.

**19. I saw none of the other apostles during this time however, except for James, the Lord's brother.**

By James, Paul is not referring to the son of Zebedee and the brother of John the Apostle, who is killed by order of Herod in Acts 12:1-2, but James the biological brother of Jesus (cf. Mk. 6:3). Although the gospels never mention him following Jesus during the time of his ministry, at some point he seems to have become a witness to the resurrection (1 Cor. 15:7) and a leader in the early Jerusalem church (cf. Acts 15:13-21, 21:18).

**20. I assure you before God that what I'm writing is no lie.**

Such was the extent to which others claimed Paul's gospel was taught to him by other apostles that Paul feels the need to follow up his statements with an emphatic oath that he is not lying.

**21-22. From there I went into Syria and Cilicia where I was personally unknown to the churches of Christ in Judea.**

Following his brief time in Jerusalem, Paul went into Syria and Cilicia, i.e., Antioch and Tarsus.

**24. And they glorified God in me.**

Paul reminds his readers that the Judean churches had once glorified God for his work among the Gentiles, implying that their recent conflicts were not really about the specifics of Paul's teaching, but about a change in the churches stance toward non-Jewish believers.

**1. Then after fourteen years, I went up to Jerusalem again, only this time with Barnabas and Titus.**

Paul's point here is that for fourteen years he had no direct dealings with the churches of Judea or its leaders; presumably because he was engaged in his mission to the Gentiles, for which the church at Antioch served as his primary base of operations (cf. Acts 13:1-3).

Paul's traveling companions on this trip are noteworthy. Barnabas (meaning "son of encouragement"), a devout Jewish believer, and leading member in the early church (cf. Acts 4:36-37), is described in Acts as an early supporter of Paul's, and possibly even a mentor:

> But Barnabas took him and brought him to the apostles. He told them how Saul on his journey had seen the Lord and that the Lord had spoken to him, and how in Damascus he had preached fearlessly in the name of Jesus. (Acts 9:27)

Unlike Barnabas, a prominent Jew, Titus was an uncircumcised Greek, and likely a convert of Paul's own (cf. Titus 1:4). His presence in Jerusalem would have served as a proof of Paul's Gentile mission and evidence of the real fruit of his preaching. As Martin Luther put it:

> By presenting himself with both Barnabas and Titus, Paul would show that he was at liberty to be a Gentile with Titus and a Jew with Barnabas. Proving the freedom of the gospel in each case...[9]

---

[9]  Martin Luther, paraphrased from citation in Betz, *Galatians*, 84n. 252.

## 2. I went in response to a revelation and set before them the gospel I preach among the Gentiles.

Paul states that he went to Jerusalem "in response to a revelation" (kata apokalupsin). If this is the same Jerusalem visit written about in Acts 15, then one must reconcile Paul's claim that the visit was undertaken in response to revelation, and Acts 15:2, which states that Paul and Barnabas undertook the journey because they were "appointed" to do so by the Antioch church.

"Revelation" is likely a reference to the continued work of the Holy Spirit in and through the revelatory gifts in the church, which would make being sent by revelation and being sent by the church nearly synonymous, cf. Acts 13:1-3, where Paul and Barnabas are set apart for missionary work by the Holy Spirit, and then subsequently sent out by the Antiochene church.

## Though privately with those esteemed – lest I be found running or to have run in vain.

Paul held no doubts about the divine origin of his message, or God's initiative in calling him to bring Jews and Gentiles into one family. If the apostles in Jerusalem had rejected his mission out of hand, however, it would have been as if he were running, or had run his race in vain.

## 3. Not even Titus, who had accompanied me, was compelled to be circumcised.

That Titus, Paul's Greek companion, was not compelled to be circumcised was evidence of the Jerusalem church's acceptance, at least on some level, of Paul's practice of receiving uncircumcised Gentiles into the church.

When Paul states that Titus was not "compelled" to undergo physical circumcision he is using the same verb (anangkazo) that he uses in 2:14 ("why do you *compel* Gentiles to live as Jews?", NKJV) and 6:12 ("these would *compel* you to be circumcised", NKJV), linking the Jerusalem meeting (2:1-10) to the controversy at Antioch (2:11-21), as well as the current situation in Galatia (6:12-13).

**4. This only became an issue because of false brothers who came in among us.**

Paul likely regards his opponents, who were themselves Jewish Christians, as "false brothers" because they championed a version of the gospel that he himself regarded as false (cf. Gal. 1:6-9).

Luke describes them in Acts as "believers who belonged to the sect of the Pharisees" (Acts 15:5, NLT), meaning they were Christians [followers of Christ] who continued to staunchly uphold the Law and the Pharisaic traditions.

**6-7. As for those who were esteemed...they added nothing to me.**

By "those who were esteemed," Paul has in mind James, Cephas [Peter] and John, who were apparently the key leaders in the Jerusalem church.

By "added nothing," Paul likely means that they added nothing to his standing as an apostle or to his articulation of the gospel. Nor did they insist that he add to or take anything from his message.

**But recognized that I was entrusted with the gospel to the uncircumcised, just as Peter had been among the circumcision.**

Despite being called to minister in vastly different cultural settings, it was the same God at work in both Peter and Paul; the same God who had "entrusted" each with the gospel; and the same God whose grace was being manifested through each of their ministries.

> There are different kinds of gifts, but the same Spirit distributes them. There are different kinds of service, but the same Lord. There are different kinds of working, but in all of them and in everyone it is the same God at work. (1 Cor. 12:4-6, NIV)

**8. For the One who worked in Peter as an apostle among the circumcised, was now working in me also among the nations.**

Paul sees him and Peter as complimentary instruments laboring on behalf of a common gospel (cf. 1 Cor. 3:5-9). Two generals heading up missions by which the one gospel is making its way to the whole world.

**9. When they saw the grace that had been given to me, [they] extended to Barnabas and I the right hand of fellowship.**

By "the right hand of fellowship," Paul is signifying that he and Barnabas were recognized as laboring in a common venture with the Judean church and sharing with them in a common faith.

**Agreeing that we should work among the Gentiles, and they among the circumcised.**

In effect, the agreement struck in Jerusalem acknowledged a separate-but equal Gentile mission, while allowing the Judean church to maintain its focus on the Jews.

The agreement presupposed the existence of a common gospel but acknowledged the need for separate missions and communities. Still, Paul seems to have believed that the Judean churches would now acknowledge the equality and free fellowship of Jews and Gentiles in Christ, allowing for mixed gatherings, worship, and meals among believers of all ethnicities (cf. Gal. 3:28).[10]

While there appears to have been agreement on the surface, many of the stricter Torah-observant Christians had interpreted the compromise in far less liberal terms than Paul.

As time would prove, the agreement had not gone nearly as far as it needed to in clarifying the relationship between Jewish and Gentile believers in mixed congregations, such as those in Antioch or Galatia. As a result, there was no real consensus regarding social relations and table fellowship between Jewish and Gentile Christians.

---

[10] Hays, *Galatians* (2000)

**10. All they asked was that we remember the poor, the very thing I was already determined to do.**

Several references in Paul's letters show that this monetary collection for the poor in Judea became a major part of his ministry among the non-Jewish churches (cf. Rom 15:25-27, 1 Cor 16:1-4, 2 Cor. 8-9).

Paul understood this offering "for the poor among the Lord's people in Jerusalem" as a sign of the spiritual solidarity held between the Gentile congregations and the Jerusalem church (Rom. 15:26-27, NIV). He here points out their request that he remember the poor [specifically the poor among God's people in Judea], confident that he has kept his part of the agreement.

# III. Crucified with Christ

## Galatians 2:11–21

[11] But when Cephas came to Antioch, I opposed him to his face, because he stood condemned. [12] For before certain men sent by James came to Antioch, he would eat with the Gentiles. But when they arrived, he began drawing back and separating himself out of fear of the circumcision. [13] The other Jews joined him in his hypocrisy, until finally even Barnabas was caught up in it.

[14] When I saw that they were not walking in line with the truth of the gospel, I said to Cephas in front of them all, "You're a Jew, and yet you live like a Gentile and not a Jew. So why are you compelling Gentiles to Judaize?

[15] For we who were born Jews and not Gentile sinners [16] know that a person isn't justified by works of the Law, but through the faith of Jesus Christ. We too have put our faith in Christ that we might be justified by the faith of Christ and not the works of the Law – for no flesh can be justified by works of the Law!

[17] But if we are found in sin, even while saying we are justified in Christ, does that mean that Christ is the minister of sin? Absolutely not! [18] But if I rebuild what I've already torn down, then I myself am the transgressor.

[19] For through the Law I died to the Law, that I might live unto God. [20] I was crucified with Christ and now live, yet not I, but Christ lives in me. And the life I now live in the flesh, I live through the faith of the Son of God, who loved me and gave himself for me. [21] I will not set aside the grace

of God, for if righteousness is gained through the Law, then Christ died for nothing!"

---

## 11. But when Cephas came to Antioch...

To understand the importance of Antioch, as well as the significance of Peter's visit there, one should bear in mind that Antioch was the third largest city in the Roman empire (after Rome and Alexandria).[11] At some point in the past, Antioch had become home to a large Jewish population which had the distinction of freely mixing with its non-Jewish neighbors. According to Josephus, the Jewish community attracted large numbers of Gentile "godfearers" to its synagogue, who were drawn to the worship of the one God, while never fully converting to Judaism, i.e., *becoming Jews*. As Josephus writes...

> They were constantly attracting to their religious ceremonies multitudes of Greeks, and these they had in some measure incorporated with themselves.[12]

It was at Antioch that Jewish Christians first began to preach extensively to Gentile converts, with the church there eventually becoming a major base of operations for what some later called Gentile Christianity (cf. Acts 11:19-26, 13:1-3).

---

[11] Longenecker, R.N., Galatians (1990)
[12] Josephus, *The Jewish War* 7.43, 45.

Some of the believers who went to Antioch from Cyprus and Cyrene began preaching to the Gentiles about the Lord Jesus. The Lord's power was with them, and many Gentiles believed and turned to the Lord. When the Jerusalem church heard what had happened, they sent Barnabas to Antioch... Then Barnabas went to Tarsus to find Saul [Paul]. When he found him, he brought him back with him to Antioch, where they stayed with the church for a full year, teaching large numbers of people. It was here at Antioch that the disciples were first called "Christians." (Acts 19:20-25)

A unique distinctive of the Christian church at Antioch was that its members regularly took meals together at a common table. This reflected their conviction that participation in the life and community of God was determined by God's grace alone, mediated through the death of Jesus Christ, and not ethnically defined marks of covenant membership, such as *circumcision, New Moons, Sabbaths,* and *food laws.*

*One gospel = one people = one table.*

Paul does not explain exactly how those "sent by James" exerted pressure on Peter to stop eating with non-Jewish believers, only that he himself refused to tolerate Peter's inconsistency.

**I opposed him to his face.**

Paul opposed Peter "to his face" (v. 11) in a very public display ("in front of them all," v. 14) at Antioch.

**Because he stood condemned.**

The previously unified church in Antioch had now been split into two different ethnic communities and tables with Torah observance as the dividing wall between them. From Paul's perspective, God's judgment on Peter's public denial of his reconciling grace was clear: "he stood condemned."

## 12. He would eat with the Gentiles…he began drawing back…

Paul's use of the imperfect verb ("he would eat") implies that Peter's habit of eating with non-Jews in Antioch had been a regular practice engaged in over time.

By "drawing back" (hupostellō), Paul is implying that Peter was engaged in a tactical retreat, like an army pulling back from an exposed position.[13]

**Out of fear of the circumcision.**

By "fear of the circumcision," Paul is implying that Peter was caving into pressure from members of a particular party or faction within the Jerusalem church who focused on maintaining a distinct Jewish identity.

> So when Peter went up to Jerusalem, those of the circumcision contended with him, saying, "You went in among uncircumcised men and ate with them." (Acts 11:2-3)

## 13. The other Jews joined him in his hypocrisy, until finally even Barnabas was caught up in it.

---

[13] Betz, *Galatians* (1979)

Peter's withdrawal from the common table of Jewish and Gentile fellowship resulted in what Paul describes as a kind of mass hypocrisy. In Greek a *hupokritēs* was an actor, someone who wore a mask and played a role.

The charge ("hypocrisy!") is one which even Barnabas was "carried away with" (KJV), leaving Paul alone to argue on behalf of the new creation community which God was establishing through the gospel.

### 14. When I saw that they were not walking in line with the truth of the gospel.

The "truth of the gospel" was not merely a doctrine or creed, but a social reality. A truth that was to be embodied in the lived practices of a community. This truth was being violated by the exclusionary social practices of those who were championing a policy of separate tables.

Paul saw in their rejection of God's grace among the Gentiles, a failure to "walk in line with" (orthopodeō) the truth of the gospel itself.

### Why are you compelling Gentiles to Judaize?

The verb *ioudaizein* ("Judaize") does not necessarily mean converting to Judaism, but rather, adopting Jewish practices or behaviors, i.e., living like a Jew ceremonially. The pressure being exerted on Gentile Christians to conform to Jewish dietary norms was, for Paul, a betrayal of the gospel itself.

### 15. We who were born Jews and not Gentile sinners.

For Torah-observant Jews, even Gentiles who exercised exceptional morality were "sinners," because they remained outside of the covenant people. And to live outside of the covenant people and their relation to God, even if one has virtue in every other respect, is to remain in sin.

## 16. A person isn't justified by works of the Law...

That we are justified by the faith of Jesus Christ, and not by works of the Law is presented by Paul as "the common belief of Jewish Christians...the heart of the message of Galatians, the gospel in a nutshell."[14]

To be "justified" (dikaioō) was to be declared innocent or in the right ("righteous") with God. But for Israel's prophets and psalmists the term also bore a future connotation as well. Though we may suffer in the present, the inspired writers continually point us toward God's redemptive grace as the source of future vindication.

While Martin Luther took "works" to mean all human striving to please God, Paul's uses it as a technical term for works prescribed by Torah ("works of the Law"), specifically those which act as boundary markers of Jewish ethnic distinctiveness, i.e., circumcision, food laws, sabbath keeping, etc.

**But through the faith of Jesus Christ.**

---

[14] Hays, *Galatians*, p. 236

The phrase "through the faith of Jesus Christ" (dia pisteōs Iēsou Christou) is semantically ambiguous. Is Paul referring to the faith which we place in Jesus, or to the faithfulness which Jesus demonstrates in dying for our sins?

To begin with, in Greek the word "faith" (pistis) isn't simply a synonym for "belief," but can also mean "confidence," "trust," "fidelity," or "faithfulness." Rarely does *pistis* (or its Hebrew equivalent, *emūnāh*) imply cognitive belief in an idea or doctrine. Rather, it is the trust or confidence that one places in a person, particularly God.

The reading of Galatians in this commentary is based on the understanding that *pisteōs Iēsou Christou* means "the faithfulness of Jesus Christ" in giving himself for our sins (1:4).[15] Paul seems to affirm this reading in v. 21, where he insists that righteousness comes through the death of Christ.

### No flesh can be justified by works of the Law!

Paul here echoes Psalm 143:2, *"for no one living is righteous before you" (NIV).*

The point is that no human being can stand before God's judgement and declare themselves just. Real hope, even for those "born as Jews," rests in the redemptive grace and power of God and not human works, Law, or ethnic identity.

---

[15] Hays, Galatians, p. 240

**17. But if we are found in sin, even while saying we are justified in Christ, does that mean that Christ is the minister of sin?**

Paul's line of reasoning here is this: If Jews who eat with Gentiles become "sinners" by associating with them at table, then Christ, who is responsible for bringing Jews and Gentiles together, is himself aiding and abetting sin by acting as its servant or "table-waiter."

**18. If I rebuild what I've already torn down, then I myself am the transgressor.**

The "I" throughout vv. 18-21 is a representative "I." Yes, Paul is speaking in the first person, and the verses reflect his own thoughts and feelings, but Paul is also inviting his readers to join with him in his confessional union with Christ, and to acknowledge for themselves everything that this union really implies.

For Paul, this union was to be the common experience of all those who received the gospel in faith. To rebuild the old fixtures and erect the old boundary lines that separated us from one another, was to set aside God's grace in favor of the very world that Christ had died to set us free from (1:4).

Paul's imagery of tearing down and rebuilding suggests that the Law functioned as a kind wall separating Israel from everyone else. This coincides with depictions of the Law in 2nd century Judaism.

> Now our Lawgiver…surrounded us with impregnable gates and iron walls, that we might

not mingle at all with any of the other nations, but remain pure in body and soul, free from all vain imaginations, worshiping the one Almighty God above all creation.[16]

By pressuring Jewish Christians to distance themselves from Gentile believers at meals, those who came to Antioch were asking them to rebuild the very walls they had already torn down. Walls which Paul argues had already been destroyed by Christ.

> He united Jews and Gentiles into one people when, in his own body on the cross, he broke down the wall of hostility that separated us. He did this by ending the system of law with its commandments and regulations. He made peace between Jews and Gentiles by creating in himself one new people from the two groups. (Eph. 2:14-15, NLT)

### 19. I died to the Law, that I might live unto God.

Paul's point is that his union with Christ has effectively released him from the Law which had governed his earthly experiences in the past.

Having died and been raised to life in Israel's Messiah, he was now free to "live unto God," unburdened by the ethnic and cultural boundary markers of this world.

> Or do you not know that all of us who have been baptized into Christ Jesus have been baptized into His death? Therefore we have been buried with him

---

[16] *The Letter of Aristeas 139-140* (3rd – 2nd Century BC)

through baptism into death, so that, just as Christ was raised from the dead through the glory of the Father, so we too may walk in newness of life. (Rom. 6:3-4, NASB)

## 20. I was crucified with Christ and now live, yet not I, but Christ lives in me.

When Paul says he was "crucified with Christ" the verb "crucified" is perfect tense, signifying a past action with ongoing effects in the present.

For Paul, the crucifixion wasn't just an event in history, but a reality which continued to shape his experience in the present.

### I live through the faith of the Son of God.

Paul is not here saying that he lives by "believing in" Christ, but rather, that the self-giving faithfulness of God's Son now lives within him, manifesting itself through his life and actions.

### Who loved me and gave himself for me.

The words "loved" and "gave" both refer to the love enacted by Jesus on the cross – *a love made manifest in action and in suffering.*[17]

For God so loved the world that he gave his only son… (Jn. 3:16)

And this is how we know what love is: Jesus Christ laid down his life for us. (1 Jn. 3:16)

---

[17] Hays, *Galatians*, p. 244

God demonstrates his love for us in this way: That while we were still sinners, Christ died for us. (Rom. 5:8)

**21. I do not set aside the grace of God, for if righteousness is gained through the Law, then Christ died for nothing!**

In the final verse of the letter's opening argument Paul summarizes all that has been said up to this point: Righteousness – *the status of God's covenant people* – cannot be earned by ceremonial observance, ethnic descent, culture, or acts of religion, but through the self-giving love of God's Son on the cross.

Leaving no room for personal boasting or works, what God offers us in their place is a righteousness based on grace alone. For Gentile believers, however, to Judaize, i.e., pursue righteousness by becoming ceremonial Jews, would be to "set aside the grace of God" and render the death of Christ a meaningless event.

# IV. Spirit, Works, and Faith

## Galatians 3:1–14

**3** O foolish Galatians! Who has set this spell on you, before whose very eyes Jesus Christ was shown crucified? **²** This one thing I want to learn from you: Did you receive the Spirit by obeying the Law, or by the hearing of faith? **³** Are you really this foolish? Having already begun in the Spirit, are you now trying to make yourselves whole by means of your flesh? **⁴** Have you experienced all these things for nothing – if it really is for nothing? **⁵** Is God giving you the Spirit and performing acts of power among you through the working of the Law, or through the hearing of faith?

**⁶** Abraham also "believed God, and it was counted to him for righteousness." **⁷** I want you to know that those of faith are the true children of Abraham. **⁸** And Scripture, foreseeing that God would justify the Gentiles by faith, announced the gospel to Abraham afore, saying: "All nations will be blessed through you." **⁹** So those of faith are blessed with faithful Abraham.

**¹⁰** But those relying on works of the Law are under a curse, as it is written. "Cursed are those who do not continue to do the things written in the Book of the Law." **¹¹** That none are justified by Law before God is evident, for "the just shall live by faith." **¹²** And the Law is not of faith; but rather, "the one who does these things shall live by them." **¹³** Christ has redeemed us from the curse of the Law by bearing the curse for us, for it is written: "Cursed is everyone who hangs upon a beam." **¹⁴** That the blessing of Abraham might come to the Gentiles in Christ Jesus, and that we might receive the promise of the Spirit by faith.

---

### 1. O foolish Galatians! Who has set this spell on you (?)

The verb to "set a spell on" or "bewitch" (NIV) likens the false teaching of the anti-gospel to witchcraft or sorcery, and the teachers themselves to malevolent spell casters seeking to blind the Galatians to the truth of the crucifixion and its effects, as if by magic.

### Before whose very eyes Jesus Christ was shown crucified?

The word "shown" (prographō) literally means to be written or designated before. Paul's point is that Jesus had already been set forth before the Galatians as one whose identity was inextricably marked by his death on the cross.

> For I resolved to know nothing while I was with you except Jesus Christ and him crucified. (1 Cor. 2:2, NIV)

Perhaps the biggest problem with the false teachers was that their "gospel," seeing as it insisted on circumcision and Law observance for non-Jews, denied the world-changing power of Christ's death altogether.

### 2. Did you receive the Spirit by obeying the Law, or by the hearing of faith?

This is Paul's first reference in Galatians to the Spirit, which his readers had received *ex akoēs pisteōs* ("by the hearing of faith.") – not "works."

For Paul, receiving the Holy Spirit was the real proof that one had been set apart and adopted into God's family. Both here and in the book of Acts, "receiving the Spirit" is a perceivable experience; a phenomenon so vivid that it is unquestionable to the one experiencing it.

Just as Paul argued that no one could be justified by ceremonial observance, ethnic descent, or acts of religion, he now asks his readers if they had received the Spirit by any of these means either.

**3. Having already begun in the Spirit, are you now trying to make yourselves whole by means of your flesh?**

Paul here scoffs at the notion that having received the Spirit of God, his readers could now improve upon their lot by cutting off the foreskin of their flesh, or adopting Israel's ethnic and cultural norms.

**4. Have you experienced all these things for nothing (?)**

Paul's point here is that the Galatians, by accepting the requirements of circumcision and Jewish Law, were invalidating the meaning and power of their own experience of the Spirit.

**5. Is God giving you the Spirit and performing acts of power among you through the working of the Law, or through the hearing of faith?**

Paul's wording suggests that the Galatians had continued to experience the Spirit among them. In writing, he uses the present tense to describe both the supply of the Spirit and the working of power among them.

The emphasis in Paul's writing is on God's agency and initiative in freely giving the Spirit to those in Christ. The idea that the self-initiated action of God can be prompted or demanded because of our human works or Torah-observance is foolishness to Paul.

**6. Abraham also "believed God, and it was counted to him for righteousness."**

Paul's opponents had almost surely used Genesis 17 in their teaching and appeal to the Galatians. This is the chapter in Genesis where Abraham receives and obeys the command to circumcise himself and all the males born in his home.

By focusing on an earlier period of Abraham's life, Paul demonstrates that Abraham's story was not fundamentally about his circumcision and obedience; but rather, his faith (trust/belief) in God's promise (Gen. 15:6).

**7. I want you to know that those of faith are the true children of Abraham.**

Though circumcision was the distinguishing mark of the Jew, Abraham was still uncircumcised when he came to faith, and therefore a kind of Gentile himself when God declared him righteous (Gen. 15:6).

His circumcision, which happened 14 years later, was an outward mark in his flesh confirming, but not conferring his covenant status. In other words, his circumcision added nothing to the righteousness that God had already conferred on him through faith.

Paul language suggests that faith is the real identifier for those in Abraham's family, not circumcision which came later. Abraham's true children are *"faith people,"* meaning those who believe as opposed to *"circumcision people,"* meaning those defined by ethnic or cultural markers.

**8. And Scripture, foreseeing that God would justify the Gentiles by faith, announced the gospel to Abraham afore, saying: "All nations will be blessed through you."**

According to Paul, the "gospel" announced to Abraham in the past involved the promise that every nation would be blessed through him.

> And in you all the families of the earth will be blessed. (Gen 12:3, NASB)

> …and in him all the nations of the earth will be blessed. (Gen. 18:18, NASB)

And in your seed all the nations of the earth shall be blessed. (Gen. 22:18, NASB)

Apparently, this early articulation of God's covenant purpose did not mention Jesus by name. Instead, the "gospel" announced was articulated in terms of God's blessing to the world through Abraham and his "seed" (cf. 3:16).

**9. So those of faith are blessed with faithful Abraham.**

Paul here describes Abraham as the one who is "faithful" (pistō). But what does that mean in the context of Paul's writing? And how should we understand "faithfulness" in an argument about faith and works?

The answer is really a simple one: Abraham believed God – *"against all hope, he held to hope and believed" (Rom. 4:18)* – and for Paul, his belief constitutes his faithfulness.

It follows then that Abraham's seed (child/children) are those whose identities are shaped by the faith/trust they have in God, and not on the "works" they do in his name, just as Abraham believed/trusted in God before them.

If you are [truly] Abraham's children, then do the things that Abraham did and follow his example. (Jn. 8:39)

**10. Those relying on works of the Law are under a curse.**

Paul is not referring to the undoability of the Mosaic Law, as has often been supposed. The Law of Moses made ample provision for those who had transgressed its commandments and sinned. It did so through means such as repentance, sacrificial offerings, and the annual Day of Atonement (Yom Kippur).

What Paul is referring to as a "curse" is a life lived under the dichotomy of curses and blessings in the Mosaic Law. Not because some measure of obedience was impossible, but because Israel was already under the punishment of exile – which they were still living under spiritually – for their continued failures.

**Cursed are those who do not continue to do the things written in the Book of the Law.**

Paul is here quoting from Deut. 27:26 and possibly Deut. 28:58.

> Cursed is anyone who does not uphold the words of this law by carrying them out. (Deut. 27:26, NIV)

> If you do not carefully follow all the words of this law, which are written in this book…the LORD will send fearful plagues on you and your descendants. (Deut. 28:58-59, NIV)

**11. The just shall live by faith.**

Paul has been arguing that "faith" and "works of Law" are incompatible sources of identity for those in Christ. One must either define themselves by one or the other, meaning works or faith!

For its part, the Law did not have the power to give its devotees life or set them in a right relationship with God. The only way that the "just" would truly find life, Paul argues, is by *faith* (cf. Hab. 2:4).

## 12. The Law is not of faith...

To live under Law (Torah) is to live in a world where a "curse" hangs over the head of all those who violate its standard. A world where the land itself threatens to "vomit you out" if you fail to uphold the righteous standard of God's decrees (cf. Lev. 18:28).

**The one who does these things shall live by them.**

Paul's here uses a quotation from Lev. 18:5 to demonstrate the hollow promise of the Law. Verses 11 and 12 are a contrast between the one who lives "by doing" and the one who lives "by faith."

## 13. Christ has redeemed us from the curse of the Law by bearing the curse for us.

The word "redeemed" is the same word used by ancient writers to describe the emancipation of a slave. In Jesus, a mysterious pattern of redemption is unfolded and enacted on our behalf. One in which Jesus enters Israel – *as Israel* – absorbing the fulness of the curse pronounced by the Law, i.e., being treated as if he were accursed, and exhausting its penalty in himself.

This is the mystery that stands at the heart of Paul's proclamation of the gospel, a mystery which effectively takes us from the present evil age (cf. 1:4) into the grace and blessing of the age to come.[18]

## "Cursed is everyone who hangs upon a beam."

Paul lifts this phrase from Deut. 21:23, lit. *"for he that hangs is accursed of God."* The reference in the original is to the exposure of the body upon a beam or stake after death.

## 14. That the blessing of Abraham might come to the Gentiles in Christ Jesus.

Christ taking the curse of the Law upon himself is here revealed as the redemptive act that allows the blessing of Abraham to finally flow to the "nations of the earth" (cf. vv. 8-9).

## That we might receive the promise of the Spirit by faith.

Paul now ties the Abrahamic blessing to the nations and the Messianic redemption of Israel to the outpouring of God's Spirit on both Jews and Gentiles alike.

Part of the way he does this is by alluding to the prophetic texts that promise both the restoration of Israel and the ingathering of the Gentiles (e.g., Isa. 2:2-4, 60:1-22). For the prophets, these promises were uniquely tied to the outpouring of God's Spirit (Isa. 32:15-17, 44:1-5, 59:21, Ezek. 11:14-21, 36:22-27, 37:1-14). Paul thence sees the Spirit, and those filled with it, as visible proofs of God's

---

[18] cf. "Such an awesome mystery can only be proclaimed, not explained." (Hays, R., 2000, p. 60)

redemption, blessing, and promise carried out through Jesus.

> I will pour out my Spirit on your offspring, and my blessing on your descendants. (Isa. 44:3, NIV)

> I will pour out my Spirit on all flesh. (Joel 2:28)

# V. The Law and The Promise

## Galatians 3:15–29

[15] Brothers, I am speaking in human terms. If a man ratifies a covenant no one would set it aside or add to it. [16] In the same way, promises were made to Abraham and his seed. It does not say to his "seeds," as if to many, but "to your seed," as if to one – *and that one is Christ.* [17] The Law, which was 430 years later, did not annul the covenant already established or nullify God's promises to Abraham. [18] But if the inheritance promised by God depends on the Law, then the promise is of no effect, even though it was by promise that God gave it.

[19] Why then was the Law given? It was given because of transgressions, but only until the Seed of promise had come, and only through angels and the hand of a mediator. [20] Now a mediator is not a *mediator* of one, but God is one.

[21] Is the Law then opposed to God's promise? No! For if it were possible for a law to impart life, then righteousness would have come from the Law. [22] But the Scripture declares that all are under sin, so that what was promised afore through the faith of Jesus Christ, might be given to those who believe.

[23] Before the coming of faith, however, we were shut in by the Law, bound until the faith was revealed. [24] So the Law became our guardian, but only until the coming of Christ, that we might be justified by faith. [25] And seeing as faith has now come, we are no longer under a guardian.

[26] For all of you are sons of God through the faith of Christ Jesus. [27] And as many of you as were baptized into Christ

have been clothed with Christ. ²⁸ So there is no longer Jew or Gentile, slave or free, male and female. Rather, you are all one in Christ Jesus. ²⁹ And if you are Christ's, then you are Abraham's seed, and heirs according to the promise.

---

### 15. I am speaking in human terms.

Paul understands that his analogy is imperfect and that his figurative language might lead some to misinterpret his writing. He therefore reminds his readers that he is speaking in a "human way," cf. "I am using human terms, because of the weakness of your flesh" (Rom. 6:19).

In writing he narrows his words and use of analogy to the understanding of his readers. As he sometimes notes, this often requires the use of imperfect language and metaphors.

### If a man ratifies a covenant no one would set it aside or add to it.

Paul is arguing that by superimposing requirements of the Law over God's promises his opponents were effectively "setting aside" (atheteō) the promises altogether, cf. *"I will not set aside (atheteō) the grace of God"* (2:21).

### 16. Promises were made to Abraham and his seed.

The word "seed" is a collective noun in both Genesis and Galatians, and a referent for Abraham's descendants, as well as Christ himself, and those incorporated into his life and body.

> And if you are Christ's, then you are Abraham's seed, and heirs according to the promise. (Gal. 3:29)

## 17. The Law, which was 430 years later, did not annul the covenant already established.

The Law came into being 430 years after God's covenant with Abraham (cf. Ex. 12:40-41), and therefore could not annul the earlier covenant or its promises.

## 18. The inheritance promised by God...

Paul frequently uses the words "righteousness" and "inheritance" to point to the status of those who now share in the covenantal blessings of Abraham, are in right standing with God, and have the gift of the Holy Spirit dwelling within them by faith.

> If *righteousness* is gained through the Law, then Christ died for nothing. (Gal. 2:21)

> If the *inheritance* promised by God depends on the Law, then the promise is of no effect. (Gal. 3:18)

## 19. Why then was the Law given?

Paul is clear that we do not receive God's Spirit through the Law (vv. 2-5), nor does the Law impart life or righteousness (vv. 11-12) or add to the Abrahamic blessing (vv. 15-18). Why then was it given? Paul's answer, though direct, is somewhat obscure.

## It was given because of transgressions.

Paul may have in mind the Law's role of naming and exposing sin itself as a transgression against God's will, cf. "where there is no law there is no transgression" (Rom. 4:15, NIV), "through the law we become conscious of our sin" (Rom. 3:20, NIV).

**But only until the Seed of promise had come.**

Paul is clear that the Law's function was temporal and tied to the present age (1:4) from which Christ has now delivered us by his death. Though the Law served its role in the world, when the true heir was revealed, and the inheritance received, the Law itself was made obsolete.

**Only through angels and the hand of a mediator.**

The phrase "through angels" suggests that angelic forces functioned as intermediary agents in the giving of the Law, cf. *"the law that was given through angels"* (Acts 7:53, NIV), *"the message spoken through angels"* (Heb. 2:2).

The phrase "the hand of a mediator" is a reference to Moses, who received the Law on Sinai and transmitted it to Israel as the one who mediated between the nation and God, cf. Ex. 20:18-21.

**20. Now a mediator is not a *mediator* of one, but God is one.**

Paul's affirmation that "God is one" echoes the *Shema*, the unifying confession of Israel's faith (Deut. 6:4). For

Paul, one God (v. 20) and one seed (v. 16) meant there could only be one people (v. 28).

## 21. Is the Law then opposed to God's promise?

If the Law had been intended by God as an agent of life and righteousness, then one could argue that it offered a rival system of salvation – one which was opposed to the promise of God.

Paul argues, however, that the Law had no power to save or impart life to others, cf. Rom. 8:3. By denying the life-giving power of the Law, Paul is not opposing the Law as such, but affirming that its true purpose was never to give life to sinners.[19]

## 22. The Scripture declares that all are under sin.

Paul here uses the word "Scripture" as a virtual synonym for "Law," giving it the same role he gives to it in Romans.

> No one will be declared righteous in God's sight by the works of the law; rather, through the law we become conscious of our sin. (Rom. 3:19-20, NIV)

## 23. The Law became our guardian...

By "guardian" (lit. "child-leader"), Paul is emphasizing the restraining and protecting function of the Law. In the Roman world a "guardian" was often a slave charged with safeguarding the life and morals of children until they were of age. In the same way, the Law played a constructive but temporary role in the life of God's

---

[19] Hays (2000), p. 268

people. A role only meant to last until the revelation of the faith by which we are now justified.

## 26. For all of you are sons of God through the faith of Christ Jesus.

All the Galatian believers, without distinction, were now children (lit. "sons") of God through the faith they had in Jesus. The emphasis for Paul in v. 26 is placed on the word "all," which is the first word in the sentence in the original Greek.

His point is that through Jesus all believers – *without distinction* – were now "sons of God," which was a title used for God's elect in the Hebrew Scriptures, cf. "You are sons of the LORD your God" (Deut. 14:1), "Israel is my son" (Ex. 4:22).

Paul's assertion parallels his assertion in v. 7 that all of those marked by faith are the "children of Abraham." In both cases, what he is doing is taking a title traditionally used for Israel and extending it to include Gentile believers in Christ.

## 27. As many of you as were baptized into Christ have been clothed with Christ.

The believer's personal identification with Christ was pictured more in physical baptism than perhaps any other rite in the early church. In baptism, the believer declares that what is historically true of Jesus is now historically true of them as well.

Have you forgotten that when we were baptized into Christ Jesus we were baptized into his death? That means we were buried with him in our baptism, that just as Christ was raised from the dead by the Father's glory, we too should now live in newness of life. (Rom. 6:3-4)

To be "clothed with Christ" meant that one had been robed in the qualities and attributes of Christ as well. In such union, one is made to share in Christ's divine sonship, as well as his death and resurrection.

## 28. There is no longer Jew or Gentile, slave or free, male and female.

In the new creation ushered in by the resurrection the ethnic and social distinctions that characterize our existence in the "present evil age" (1:4) are each stripped of their power to divide or oppress.

The radical vision offered by Paul in v. 28 foreshadows the life and spirit of the coming age. As he does in other places, Paul encourages his readers to live in the midst of the present world as if they too had been crucified (with Christ) and risen in the next.

May I never boast except in the cross of our Lord Jesus Christ, through which the world has been crucified to me, and I to the world. (Gal. 6:14, NIV)

I have been crucified with Christ and I no longer live, but Christ lives in me. (Gal. 2:20, NIV)

*There is no longer Jew or Gentile.* The first "old world" division that Paul attacks is the ethnic and cultural wall that separates God's people from all others (collectively referred to as "the Nations" or "Gentiles."). In the light of the Cross, ethnic distinctions among God's people no longer mattered, only that such people were now part of a new creation.

> Neither circumcision nor uncircumcision means anything; what counts is the new creation. (Gal. 6:15, NIV)

*There is no longer slave or free.* Distinctions of social class and hierarchy are negated by the reality of new creation as well. For Paul, social class and oppressive power structures were delegitimized by the reality of the resurrection, with the familial term "children of God" making brothers and sisters out of all members of the church.

> Perhaps the reason he was separated from you for a little while was that you might have him back forever—no longer as a slave, but better than a slave, as a dear brother. He is very dear to me but even dearer to you, both as a fellow man and as a brother in the Lord. (Philemon 15-16, NIV)

*There is no longer male and female.* Paul is by no means suggesting that those in Christ cease to be men and women, or that gender roles are negated by our entry in the church. Rather, he is arguing that the perennial distinction of male and female (cf. Gen. 1:27) is no longer the determining identity marker for believers, nor a ground for status or exclusion in the church.

It is in his final clause that Paul spells out the real point of v. 28: *You are all one in Christ Jesus!*

**29. If you are Christ's, then you are Abraham's seed, and heirs according to the promise.**

Paul has already argued in v. 16 that Christ is the true seed of Abraham, and the sole heir of the Abrahamic promise. Because those baptized into Christ are also united with him in his death and resurrection, they also share in the same privileged status as Christ himself and are heirs (in Christ) according to the promise.

> Now if we are children, then we are heirs—heirs of God and co-heirs with Christ... (Rom. 8:17, NIV)

# VI. The Fulness of Time

## Galatians 4:1–11

4 Now I tell you that while the heir is still a child, he is no different from a slave, though he is lord of everything. ² Still, he is subjected to guardians and overseers until the time appointed by his father. ³ Like children, we too were subjected to the base elements of this world. ⁴ But when the fulness of time came, God sent forth his Son born of a woman, and also born under the Law ⁵ that he might redeem those who were also under the Law, and that we too might receive the adoption of sonship. ⁶ And because you are now sons, God has sent the Spirit of his Son into our hearts crying out, *"Abba*, Father." ⁷ So you are no longer a slave, but a son; and since a son, then also an heir through God.

⁸ And though at the time you did not know God, you were enslaved to things which are not really gods; ⁹ you have now come to know him—or rather to be known by him. How then are you turning back to the weak and impoverished elements of this world? Do you desire to be enslaved by them again? ¹⁰ You are observing days and months and seasons and years! ¹¹ I fear for you, that perhaps I labored for you in vain.

---

### 1-2. He is subjected to guardians and overseers until the time appointed by his father.

Paul likens the experience of an heir that is too young to manage his inheritance to a slave. Though he is lord over everything, he lacks the authority to exercise his dominion. This authority is placed in the hands of guardians and stewards until he reaches the age of maturity. What Paul is really highlighting is the temporary character of the heir's subjection until the time appointed by his father.

### 3. We too were subjected to the base elements of this world.

Paul's "we too" brings Jewish and Gentile readers together in the same plight. All humanity – Jew and Gentile alike – were *enslaved* to various principles or elemental forces (stoicheia) prior to the coming of God's Son.

### 4. But when the fulness of time came...

The expression "the fulness of time" suggests that the coming of God's Son happened precisely according to God's ordered timetable and planning. The decision to redeem creation is God's alone, and the initiative and timing are God's alone as well.

> But about that day or hour no one knows, not even the angels in heaven, nor the Son, but only the Father. (Mk. 13:21, NIV)

> He said to them: "It is not for you to know the times or dates the Father has set by his own authority. (Acts 1:7, NIV)

### Born of a woman and also born under the Law...

The phrase "born of a woman" simply means that Jesus was human (cf. Job 14:1, Matt. 11:11), while the fact that he was born "under the Law" refers to his Jewishness, cf. "Remember that Christ came as a servant to the Jews to show that God is true to the promises he made to their ancestors" (Rom. 15:8, NLT).

## 5. That he might redeem those who were also under the Law.

That Christ was born under the Law was crucial to his Messianic function, which was to redeem Israel from the curse of the Law. The verb used implies the emancipation of those enslaved.

### That we too might receive the adoption of sonship.

The initial clause of v. 5 refers to the redemption of Israel, while the second clause refers to the justification of Gentiles, leading to their adoption as God's sons. The concept of adoption in Greek denotes one's election or placement as a son, as opposed to one's natural birth. In contrast to Christ, who is uniquely God's Son (cf. "the one and only Son, who came from the Father, full of grace and truth," Jn. 1:14, NIV), all other human beings enter God's family by adoption. As Augustine wrote when providing commentary on this very verse:

> He says *adoption* so that we may clearly understand that the Son of God is unique. For we are sons of God through his generosity and the condescension of his mercy, whereas he is Son by nature, sharing the same divinity with the Father.[20]

[20] Augustine, *Epistle to the Galatians*, cited in M. J. Edwards, ed. Ancient Christian Commentary on Scripture, vol. 8 (1999)

**6. And because you are now sons, God has sent the Spirit of his Son into our hearts crying out, *"Abba, Father."***

God not only sent the Son into the world to redeem it, but because we are now sons and daughters as well, he also sent the Spirit of the Son into our hearts, enabling us to call out to God as our own Father.

The word "Abba" (Heb. "father") was often combined with the Greek word *patēr* ("father") in the worship of early non-Jewish churches. For these men and women to call God "Father" was as much a witness to the work of the Spirit as it was to call Jesus "Lord," cf., 1 Cor. 12:3.

**8-9. You were enslaved to things which are not really gods.**

Paul elsewhere acknowledges the reality of rogue spiritual forces in the world around us, i.e., non-gods called by various names, such as "lords," "demons," "principalities," and "rulers of this age" (1 Cor. 2:8, 8:5-6, 10:20-21).

Because we live in the "already, but not yet" reality of God's kingdom, these non-gods continue to exercise power in the world around us and to oppress those who will serve them.

**You have now come to know him—or rather to be known by him.**

Cf. "You only have I *known* of all the families of the earth" (Amos 3:2, ESV), "Before I formed you in the womb I *knew* you" (Jer. 1:5, ESV), "But if anyone loves God, he is *known* by God" (1 Cor. 8:3, ESV).

## How then are you turning back to the weak and impoverished elements of this world?

The "impoverished elements of this world" is likely a reference to the elemental forces (stoicheia) which make up the natural world in which we live. Paul here suggests that the Law itself was among the enslaving "elements" from which his readers were to remain free.

## 10. You are observing days and months and seasons and years!

For centuries Jewish worship revolved around the movement of the celestial bodies in the sky (e.g., sabbaths, new-moon festivals, Passover, Yom Kippur, etc.). For this reason, Paul argues that for his Gentile readers to adopt Israel's patterns of worship would almost constitute a return to their previous worship of earthly elements, such as sun worship or the observance of new moons.

On this point, Hays rightly notes that when one strips away the specific terminology and language of the Jewish festivals, what is left is not much different from other kinds of nature religion.[21]

Paul's points can be summed up as follows: "You were once enslaved to cosmic forces which are not gods. If you now choose to come under the yoke of the Mosaic

---

[21] Hays, *Galatians* (2000), p. 288

Law, you will quickly find yourselves back under the control of these same cosmic forces."

**11. I fear for you, that perhaps I labored for you in vain.**

Paul often uses the verb "labored" to describe his work in spreading the gospel (1 Cor. 4:12, 15:10, Col. 1:29), cf. *"I will be able to boast on the day of Christ that I did not run or labor in vain"* (Phil. 2:16, NIV).

# VII. A Tale of Two Covenants

## Galatians 4:12–5:1

[12] Brothers, I'm urging you, be as I am, even as I became as you are. In no way have you wronged me in this. [13] You know that it was through my own physical infirmity that I first preached the gospel to you. [14] And even though my condition in the flesh was a trial for you, you did not despise me nor reject me because of my wounds. Instead, you welcomed me as if I were an angel from God, or even Christ himself. [15] Where then is your blessing now? I am a witness of how you were, that you would have given me your very eyes if it had been possible. [16] Have I now become your enemy by telling you the truth?

[17] Their zeal for you is not for the good, but to exclude you. What they really want is for you to become zealous for them. [18] Now being zealous for a good thing is right, but all of the time and not just when I am with you. [19] O children of mine, I am laboring in birth for you all over again until Christ himself is formed among you. [20] How I wish I were with you now and could change my tone, because I'm at a loss about how to help you!

[21] Those of you who desire to be under the Law, tell me, do you know what the Law says? [22] For it is written that Abraham had two sons, one born of a slave and the other born of a free woman. [23] The son born of the slave woman was born according to the flesh, but the son born of the free woman was born through the promise.

²⁴ Now such things are symbolic, for the two women represent two covenants. One from Mount Sinai, bearing children who are slaves: This is Hagar. ²⁵ Now Hagar is Mount Sinai in Arabia and corresponds to the present Jerusalem, which is in slavery with her children. ²⁶ But the Jerusalem that is above is free, which is our mother. ²⁷ For it is written:

> "Rejoice, you who are barren and have never bore a child; break forth and cry out, you who have never been in labor, because more are the children of the desolate than of her having the husband."

²⁸ Now you, brothers, in the same manner as Isaac, are the children of promise. ²⁹ And just as then, the son born of the flesh persecuted the son born of the Spirit, so it is now. ³⁰ But what does the Scripture say? "Cast out the slave and her son, for the son of the slave will not inherit with the son of the free." ³¹ Now then, brothers, we are not children born of the slave, but of the free.

5 Stand firm then in the freedom into which Christ has released us, and do not accept another yoke of slavery.

---

## 12. Be as I am, even as I became as you are.

As part of his work as an apostle to the Gentiles Paul had already "torn down" (2:18) the barriers between him and his readers. As a result, he had fellowshipped and eaten meals with Gentiles, and even taken a stand against other Jewish Christians who refused to do so (2:11-14).

Paul's assertion that he "became" as the Galatians are should probably be understood in the context of his overall strategy for reaching Jewish and Gentile hearers with the Gospel.

> To the Jews I became like a Jew, to win the Jews. To those under the law I became like one under the law (though I myself am not under the law), so as to win those under the law. To those not having the law I became like one not having the law… I have become all things to all people so that by all possible means I might save some. I do all this for the sake of the gospel, that I may share in its blessings. (1 Cor. 9:20-23, NIV)

**13. You know that it was through my own physical infirmity that I first preached the gospel to you.**

Paul's words require us to do some guesswork here. What exactly is the "physical infirmity" (lit. "weakness or suffering of the flesh") that Paul is referring to? While we do not know for certain, a good case can be made that Paul is referring to the scars and physical injuries he sustained through persecution (6:17, Acts 14:19, 2 Cor. 6:4-5, 11:23-25) – *"let no one trouble me, for I bear in my body the marks of the Lord Jesus"* (Gal. 6:17, NKJV).

Either way, Paul's physical condition had brought him to the region of Galatia (possibly to heal from injuries he had incurred) where he first met the Galatians and preached the gospel to them, though suffering from the "infirmity" or "wounds" in his flesh.

**14. You did not despise me nor reject me because of my wounds. Instead, you welcomed me as if I were an angel from God, or even Christ himself.**

Others may have beaten him and rejected his message about Christ, but the Galatians had received him warmly, as though he were a heavenly messenger, or even Christ.

**15. Where then is your blessing now?**

Paul is asking his readers what had happened to the blessing and good will they had felt toward him. They had once rejoiced in his message about the Messiah and basked in his personal witness of Jesus. Why were they now criticizing him rather than blessing him?

**16. Have I now become your enemy by telling you the truth?**

The influence of the rival teachers in Galatia had caused Paul's readers to no longer consider him a friend, but someone with whom they were openly hostile or at enmity with.

If there is enmity, Paul states, it is only because he has insisted on telling them the truth, cf. "But we did not yield to them for even an hour, that the truth of the gospel might remain with you" (2:5).

**17. Their zeal for you is not for the good, but to exclude you.**

The zeal of the rival teachers in Galatia was duplicitous, Paul charges, and hypocritical. By excluding the Galatians from participating in full Christian fellowship, they were pressuring them to "Judaize" if they wanted to be accepted as "real" Christians. The exclusivity of their "brand" of the Christian faith may have had the effect of making it appear even more desirable. Especially to those who were now being made to feel as if they were still on the outside of the true Jesus movement.

### 19. O children of mine, I am laboring in birth for you all over again.

Paul elsewhere likens his relation to the churches he's planted to that of a father to his children (e.g., 1 Cor. 4:14-15, 1 Thess. 2:11-12). Here he changes the parental metaphor, likening himself to a mother laboring to complete an as yet unfinished birthing process.

In Jewish and early Christian eschatology, the travail leading to the final revelation of the Messiah was called *chevlei Mashiach* ("the birth pains of Messiah"). For Paul, these chevlei were not something coming in the future, but a present experience. His apostolic anguish, as Beverly Gaventa notes in her study on Galatians, reflects the anguish of the entire creation as it awaits the fulfillment of God's final revelation in Jesus Christ.[22]

### 20. I'm at a loss about how to help you!

---

[22] Gaventa, B. R., The Maternity of Paul: An Exegetical Study of Galatians 4:19 (1990)

Paul closes this section of his letter off with a note of bewilderment. The Galatians have ruptured their relationship with their apostle, and their rejection has left him stunned and puzzled, as well as at a loss for how to help them.

### 21. Those of you who desire to be under the Law...

For Paul, desiring to be "under the Law" meant that his readers now desired to make Law keeping – *instead of Christ* – the basis of their relationship with God.

### Do you know what the Law says?

The question implies that his readers' infatuation with the Law was based on their own ignorance of what the Law actually says. In the Greek, he literally asks, "Do you not hear *(attentively listen to)* the Law?"

### 22. Abraham had two sons, one born of a slave and the other born of a free woman.

Paul wants his Galatian readers to "hear" the story of Abraham's two sons (from Genesis 16-21) through new ears. In his bold retelling of the narrative, it is the uncircumcised Gentile converts, and not their Jewish born teachers, who are likened to the child of promise (v. 28).

### 23. The son born of the free woman was born through the promise.

Paul states that Abraham's first son was born "according to the flesh," whereas his second son was born through the power of God's promise, when Sarah had well passed the age of childbearing (Gen. 18:1).

## 24. Now such things are symbolic.

Cf. "being taken *figuratively*" (NIV), "serve as *illustrations*" (BSB), "are an *allegory*" (KJV). Allegory was a well-known method in the ancient world for interpreting stories as having a figurative meaning apart from their overt literal meaning.

Paul is not here stating that Genesis 16-21 is merely a symbolic story, but speaking with respect to the symbolic interpretation he is decidedly giving to it.

### The two women represent two covenants.

The "two covenants" here should not be read as "two religions" (i.e., Judaism and Christianity), but two rival interpretations of the covenant promise given to Abraham. We should also remember that both interpretations are Jewish interpretations, one from Paul and the other from the rival Jewish teachers opposing him.

## 25. Now Hagar is Mount Sinai in Arabia and corresponds to the present Jerusalem, which is in slavery with her children.

To "correspond" does not mean that Hagar and Sinai "represent" Jerusalem, but that they stand in the same position or category as the latter city. What Paul is explaining to his readers is how "Hagar" can symbolize both the covenant entered into on Sinai in Arabia and the present-day Jerusalem of his time.

For Paul, both Jerusalem and the Jerusalem church were in bondage, one to foreign powers and the other to the Law. Those converted by the Law-observant teachers were consequently in bondage to the same Law as their converters.

## 26. But the Jerusalem that is above is free, which is our mother.

The image of the "Jerusalem above" is suggested in Isaiah 54 and Ezekiel 40-48, as well as Heb. 12:22, 13:14, and Revelation 21. And the metaphor of Jerusalem as our "mother" is suggested in Isa. 50:1 and Hos. 2:2-5.

In contrast to the earthly Jerusalem, which is in slavery with her children, Paul declares that those in Christ, despite suffering trials and adversity in the present, are children of the heavenly Jerusalem which is above and free.

## 27. Rejoice, you who are barren and have never bore a child...

Paul's reference to the barren woman of Isaiah 54:1 recalls Sarah's barrenness before the birth of Isaac (the child of promise). Paul is eluding to the Jewish hope of God's restoration and connecting it to the prophesied embrace of the Gentiles. For Isaiah, the increase of the barren was associated with the nations (Gentiles) coming to acknowledge Israel's God (e.g., Isa. 49:6, 51:4-5, 52:10, 54:2-3, 55:5).

For Paul, God's gathering of the nations through Israel's Messiah is the fulfillment of His real promise to Abraham and Sarah (cf. 3:8-9, 14, 29).

## 28. Now you, brothers, in the same manner as Isaac, are the children of promise.

Paul now spells out the real implications of his allegory. His Gentile readers, in the same manner as Isaac, are now children and heirs of the promise. In fact, they are the heirs for whom the promise was destined from the first.

> And Scripture, foreseeing that God would justify the Gentiles by faith, announced the gospel to Abraham afore, saying: "All nations will be blessed through you." (Gal. 3:8)

## 29. The son born of the flesh persecuted the son born of the Spirit.

Isaac is here described as being "born of the Spirit" for the first time in Paul's letter, making him an allegorical figure for believers who now receive the Spirit and call out – *along with Christ* – "Abba, Father" (cf. 4:6-7).

## 30. What does the Scripture say?

After bringing his allegorical reading to its conclusion, Paul now allows the Hebrew Scriptures to speak directly to his readers:

> Cast out the slave and her son, for the son of the slave will not inherit with the son of the free. (Gen. 21:10)

The point of the reference is clear: Scripture itself is telling them to throw out the rival Missionaries and their converts. The inheritance belongs to the children of the free woman, the Jerusalem above, and they should not tolerate the presence of troublemakers who are trying to bring them into slavery. Rather, they should expel them from their churches immediately!

**1. Stand firm then in the freedom into which Christ has released us, and do not accept another yoke of slavery.**

The word "yoke" was often used in first century Judaism to describe the stability and guidance provided by the Scriptures and sound Rabbinic teaching (cf. "Take my yoke upon you and learn from me," Matt. 11:29). Paul here shifts the metaphor though, invoking the imagery of constraint, as well as cultural and religious domination.

> Why do you try to test God by putting on the necks of Gentiles a *yoke* that neither we nor our ancestors have been able to bear? (Acts 15:10, NIV)

Because Christ had already delivered Paul's readers from slavery to cultural and religious systems of oppression, they were never – *under any circumstances* – to tolerate being brought under the rule of such systems again!

# VIII. Life in the Spirit

## Galatians 5:2–26

² Listen! What I'm saying is that if you become circumcised then Christ will avail you nothing at all. ³ I testify again that every man who becomes circumcised is obligated to obey the whole Law. ⁴ And anyone trying to be justified by the Law is alienated from Christ; and has fallen away from grace. ⁵ But we – through the Spirit and by faith – eagerly await the hope of righteousness.⁶ For in Christ Jesus neither circumcision nor uncircumcision has any power. Only the outworking of faith through love.

⁷ You were running so well! Who hindered you from following the truth? ⁸ This influence is not from the one calling you. ⁹ But "a little leaven leavens the whole lump." ¹⁰ I am confident of you in the Lord that you will hold no other view. The one troubling you will bear the judgment, whoever he is. ¹¹ As for me, if I am still proclaiming circumcision then why am I being persecuted? For the offense of the cross would be removed. ¹² I wish your agitators would follow all the way through and cut themselves off!

¹³ Brothers, you were called into freedom. Not to indulge the flesh; but to serve each other in love. ¹⁴ For the whole Law is fulfilled in one saying: "Love your neighbor as yourself." ¹⁵ But if you bite at one another and tear at your neighbor, then take heed lest you bring one another to ruin.

¹⁶ But if you walk by the Spirit then I say to you, "you will not gratify the desire of the flesh." ¹⁷ For the flesh desires what is contrary to the Spirit, and the Spirit what is contrary

to the flesh. They oppose one another, so that you no longer do the things you might wish. [18] But if you are led by the Spirit, then you are not under the Law.

[19] Now the works of the flesh are evident, being sexual immorality, impurity, indecency, [20] idolatry, sorcery, contentions, strife, jealousy, outbursts of anger, fleshly ambitions, division, sectarianism, [21] envy, drunkenness, rioting, and the like. I warn you, as I did before, that those who live in this way will not inherit God's kingdom.

[22] But the fruit of the Spirit is love, joy, peace, patience, kindness, goodness, faithfulness, [23] gentleness and self-control. Against such things there is no law. [24] And those who now belong to Christ Jesus have crucified the flesh with its passions and desires. [25] If we live by the Spirit, then we should also walk by the Spirit,[26] and not become boastful, provoking and envying one another.

---

## 2. If you become circumcised then Christ will avail you nothing at all.

Though Paul himself was a circumcised Jewish believer (Phil. 3:5), he well understood that for non-circumcised Gentiles to become Jews and follow the Mosaic Law as a way of being "right" with God was a denial of what Christ had already done for them. Circumcision (as a means of Jewish conversion) would mean that Law keeping – *instead of Christ himself* – had now become the basis of their relationship with God.

**3. Every man who becomes circumcised is obligated to obey the whole Law.**

To be circumcised in obedience to the Law was to come under its rule, as well as the ethnic and cultural demands it placed on the individual Jew.

**4. Anyone trying to be justified by the Law is alienated from Christ; and has fallen away from grace.**

Paul's readers had already entered a covenant relationship with God through the life and mediating work of Jesus. To now seek covenant membership through Law-keeping constituted a rejection of Christ and the unique relationship already established with God through him.

**5. But we – through the Spirit and by faith – eagerly await the hope of righteousness.**

While Paul often speaks of the present "justification" or "righteousness" of those who believe (e.g., Rom. 5:1), the words "hope of righteousness" implies a future state of redemptive grace as well.

That we "eagerly await" this hope means that we joyously long for the future disclosure of God's glory among us, cf. "as you eagerly wait for our Lord Jesus Christ to be revealed" (1 Cor. 1:7), "and we eagerly await a Savior from *heaven*" (Phil. 3:20).

**6. For in Christ Jesus neither circumcision nor uncircumcision has any power. Only the outworking of faith through love.**

Paul frequently uses the words "in Christ" (en Christo) as a spatial metaphor pointing to our new existence in Jesus. In Christ, the outworking of faith through love becomes the new modus operandi of God's people.

> …through the faith of the Son of God, who loved me and gave himself for me. (Gal. 2:20)

Christ's love is defined and demonstrated by his self-giving act on the cross, which is in turn the enactment of his faith (faithfulness). His dying for us is the outworking of faith through love, and the model to which Paul calls his readers.

**7. You were running so well! Who hindered you from following the truth?**

By "running well" Paul means that his readers were progressing on the spiritual path, cf. "So run that you may obtain" (1 Cor. 9:24). But now, like runners thrown off stride by competing runners in a race, the Galatians have been diverted from the path by false teachers.

**9. "A little leaven leavens the whole lump."**

Paul is quoting a Jewish proverb to warn against the corrupting power of false teaching. He quotes the same proverb in 1 Cor. 5:6 as well, admonishing his readers to expel an unrepentant offender from the church before his influence can spread, cf. "Get rid of the old yeast, so that you may be a new unleavened batch" (1 Cor. 5:7, NIV). As in Corinth, Paul is charging the Galatians to excise the false teachers before their influence can spread.

**10. The one troubling you will bear the judgment, whoever he is.**

Paul formulates this warning in general terms, making it applicable to anyone – "whoever he is" – attempting to trouble the Galatian churches.

**11. If I am still proclaiming circumcision then why am I being persecuted? For the offense of the cross would be removed.**

Apparently, Paul's rivals were claiming that he was still preaching circumcision in some places – perhaps when it suited his purposes. The events in Acts 16, where Paul circumcises Timothy "because of the Jews in that area" would have provided some basis for this rhetoric.[23]

Paul counters that if he were preaching a "Christ plus circumcision" gospel that such preaching would have removed the "offense" (skandalon, lit. "stumbling block") of the cross, for which he was still being persecuted, cf. "but we preach Christ crucified, a stumbling block (skandalon) to the Jews" (1 Cor. 1:23).

The cross of Jesus was a stumbling block (skandalon) for many Jews because it delegitimated the distinctions

---

[23] Acts 16:1 records that Timothy's mother was Jewish, not Greek (as was his father). In Jewish tradition that made him a Jew rather than a Gentile, which may have factored into Paul's decision to circumcise him.

that gave shape to their worldview, e.g., Jew and Gentile, sacred and profane, us and them, etc.

## 12. I wish your agitators would follow all the way through and cut themselves off!

While admittedly coarse, Paul's language demonstrates the extent of the anger he felt towards those misleading the congregations he had worked so tirelessly to establish.

His words in the present verse amount to this: "If they are so eager to cut away at the male sexual organ, then I wish they would follow all the way through and completely cut themselves off."

## 13. You were called into freedom. Not to indulge the flesh; but to serve each other in love.

Throughout Galatians Paul uses the word "flesh" to denote (1) the physical body, (2) the material "stuff" from which physical bodies are made, or (3) the hostile power within physical bodies that opposes God. His point is that his readers were not to use freedom as an opportunity to indulge the hostile powers at work in their bodies.

## 14. For the whole Law is fulfilled in one saying: "Love your neighbor as yourself."

Paul here cites Leviticus 19:18 ("Love your neighbor as yourself") as the singular way the Law is fulfilled. And though it is Jesus alone who fulfills it (Matt. 5:17), Paul's readers are exhorted to participate in its fulfilling by demonstrating the kind of love that corresponds to and mirrors that of Jesus.

**15. But if you bite at one another and tear at your neighbor, then take heed lest you bring one another to ruin.**

Paul's warning suggests that the churches in Galatia may have been struggling with internal problems, such as rivalries or dissensions. The verbs in v. 15 portray an escalating conflict which left unchecked might end in their destruction of one another.

**16. If you walk by the Spirit…you will not gratify the desire of the flesh.**

Paul's rivals held that following the Law was the only way of keeping one's flesh in check. Without adhering to the Law's commandments and boundary markers they believed that men – *even those who believed in Jesus* – would eventually give in to their base desires.

Paul here argues that the community of Jesus receives its moral guidance directly from the Spirit of Christ and is under no obligation to observe the ethnic and cultural markers of Jewish Law.

**17. For the flesh desires what is contrary to the Spirit, and the Spirit what is contrary to the flesh.**

The "Spirit" referred to here by Paul is not the human spirit or ethos of the individual person, but the Spirit poured out by Jesus Christ,[24] cf. *"the Spirit of God"* (1 Cor. 2:14), *"the Spirit of Christ"* (Rom. 8:9), *"the Holy Spirit"* (2 Tim. 1:14), *"the Spirit that raised Jesus"* (Rom. 8:11), *"the Spirit of his Son"* (Gal. 4:6)*,* etc.

## 18. If you are led by the Spirit, then you are not under the Law.

Paul's central point in these verses is that it is God's Spirit who now provides guidance and direction to Christ's followers, and not the ethnic and cultural markers of the Mosaic Law.

## 19-21. Now the works of the flesh are evident.

By "evident" (phanera, lit. visible, apparent), Paul means that we do not need the "Law" to identify wrong works or behaviors, because they are obvious. He then gives an illustrative list of fifteen such works that result from a life surrendered to the flesh.

## Sexual immorality, impurity, indecency, idolatry, sorcery, contentions, strife, jealousy, outbursts of anger, fleshly ambitions, division, sectarianism, envy, drunkenness, rioting.

Paul begins his list with three terms linked to sexual offenses (immorality, impurity, indecency), continues with two words related to false worship and the occult (idolatry, sorcery), moves on to eight terms of relational offense (contention, strife, jealousy, anger, ambition, division, sectarianism, envy), and concludes with

---

[24] "He generously poured out the Spirit upon us through Jesus Christ our Savior." (Titus 3:6, NLT)

two words related to self-indulgence and partying (drunkenness, rioting).

**Those who live in this way will not inherit God's kingdom.**

The phrase "live in this way" refers to continuing action over time or habitual living, not to singular instances of sin or moral violations. Paul is referring to those who have given themselves completely over to sin.

## 22-23. The fruit of the Spirit.

The phrase "fruit of the Spirit"[25] is a harvest metaphor and reflects the outgrowth or "fruit" of God's Spirit in our lives. For Paul, the outgrowth produced by the Spirit was like the fruit of a harvest which God himself had caused to spring from the soil.

The word "fruit" (karpos) incidentally is singular, signifying a unified whole or cluster of fruit, of which each of the distinct traits outlined in vv. 22-23 form a part. The list which Paul offers his readers is illustrative (cf. "the fruit of the light," Eph. 5:8-9) and meant to serve as a counter to the various works of the flesh outlined in vv. 19-21.

> **(1) Love** (charitable, self-sacrificing, benevolent).
> **(2) Joy** (gladness, favorably disposed). **(3) Peace** (wholeness, unbrokenness, healthy). **(4) Patience** (long-suffering, enduring). **(5) Kindness** (upright, well fit for use). **(6) Goodness** (commendable,

---

[25] Cf. "fruit of the light" (Eph. 5:9)

praise worthy, of benefit). **(7) Faithfulness** (fidelity, trustworthy, believing). **(8) Gentleness** (meek, expressing power with reserve). **(9) Self-control** (mastery of oneself, restraint).

## 24. Those who now belong to Christ Jesus have crucified the flesh with its passions and desires.

For Paul, the crucifixion was both a past event and a present experience by faith. His words denote both the reality of the historical crucifixion, as well as its continuing effects in the present. Christ was crucified (past tense), and we now participate (present tense) in that crucifixion by faith.

## 25. If we live by the Spirit, then we should also walk by the Spirit.

To live by the Spirit is to walk "in step" or "in line" (stoicheó) with the will of the Spirit as well. For Paul, this meant living under the grace and influence of God and producing the fruit of his Spirit in our lives. The verses in this section make up Paul's most impassioned defense in Scripture for the sufficiency of the Spirit in guiding the community of faith.

# IX. New Creation

## Galatians 6:1–18

¹ Brothers, if anyone among you is overtaken by a transgression, then you who are spiritual should restore them in a spirit of gentleness; considering your own selves, lest you fall into temptation as well. ² For in bearing one another's burdens, you are fulfilling the Law of Christ. ³ And if anyone thinks they are something when they are not, then they are only deceiving themselves. ⁴ Let each test his own work, that their boasting may be in themselves alone, and not in comparing themselves to another, ⁵ for we must each shoulder our own burden. ⁶ Nevertheless, let those who are being taught the word share with those who are teaching them.

⁷ And be not misled, for God will not be mocked. We shall all reap whatever we've sown. ⁸ If we've sown to the flesh, then we will reap decay from the flesh; and if we've sown to the Spirit, then they will reap eternal life from the Spirit. ⁹ So let's not grow weary in our well doing, for in due time we will reap a harvest if we endure. ¹⁰ Therefore, as we have occasion, let us do good to all people, especially those belonging to the household of faith.

¹¹ Take note of the large letters in this writing, for I am writing them to you with my own hand!

¹² Those who want to make an outward showing of your flesh are compelling you to be circumcised so they can avoid persecution for the cross of Christ. ¹³ Yet not even those who are circumcised keep the Law. They only want

you circumcised so they can boast in your conversion. [14] As for me, may I never boast in anything except for the cross of our Lord Jesus Christ, through which the world has been crucified to me, and I to the world. [15] For it is neither circumcision nor uncircumcision that matters, but new creation. [16] Peace and mercy upon all those who walk by this standard, and upon the Israel of God.

[17] So from now on, let no one trouble me, for I bear in my body the marks of Jesus.

[18] Brothers, the grace of our Lord Jesus Christ be with your spirit. Amen.

---

In the final section of his letter Paul offers his readers a set of directives for walking in the Spirit, ranging from restoration of those in transgression (vv. 1-2) to self-examination (vv. 3-5) and financial support of the community's teachers (v. 6).

To be "spiritual" in the context of Galatians is to be part of the community of Jesus – those whose identities are shaped by *his Spirit*, to work towards the mending of relationships, the restoration of those hurting, and the spread of shalom (peace-wholeness-wellbeing) among people.

**1. If anyone among you is overtaken by a transgression, then you who are spiritual should restore them in a spirit of gentleness.**

Despite the Spirit's presence within the church Paul is aware of the human fallibility of its members. He charges the Galatians with restoring those overtaken by transgression in a spirit of gentleness.

The phrase "you who are spiritual" refers to all member of Christ's body – *"you who have received the Spirit" (NRSV)* – and not some hypothetical group of spiritual leaders in the church. Paul's concern is not only that correction be offered at the appropriate time, but that it be offered in the appropriate spirit as well. By "gentleness" he means that correction (or rebuke) should be offered in accordance with the fruit produced by the Spirit ("gentleness and self-control" 5:23).

**Considering your own selves, lest you fall into temptation as well.**

There is a tendency in some to most harshly judge the sins which they themselves are the most susceptible to or tempted by. Be gentle, Paul warns, and consider your own selves, lest you unwittingly fall into the same traps for which you have rebuked others.

**2. In bearing one another's burdens, you are fulfilling the Law of Christ.**

Paul wants the Galatians to know that in bearing one another's burdens[26] they are in fact fulfilling the pattern, or "Law of Christ," who took upon himself the weight

---

[26] "We who are strong ought to bear with the failings of the weak and not to please ourselves" (Rom. 15:1, NIV)

of the world's sin. His example is the source of the obligation to carry the burden of others.

### 3-5. If anyone thinks they are something when they are not... Let each test his own work...

Verses 3-5 are really a warning against boasting and spiritual pride in the church. Rather than comparing themselves to others and boasting because of some imagined sense of superiority, Paul's readers were to soberly assess their own work" and keep their boasting to themselves, cf. 2 Cor. 13:5.

> Let those who wish to boast, boast in this alone: that they have known me and that I alone am the LORD... (Jer. 9:24)[27]

> May I never boast in anything except the cross of our Lord Jesus Christ... (Gal. 6:14)

> We shall not boast beyond our limits, but within the measure of influence God has assigned to us... (2 Cor. 10:13)

### 6. Let those who are being taught the word share with those who are teaching them.

Cf. "share all good things with their instructor" (NIV), "provide for their teachers" (NLT). This verse is a directive from Paul for those in the church to provide financial support for those who carry out the ministry of teaching among them.

---

[27] Paul references Jer. 9:24 in 1 Cor. 1:31 and 2 Cor. 10:17.

Paul mentions the support of teachers because it belongs to his overall vision of a community walking under the guidance of the Spirit. The teaching he is referring to is not some dry academic exercise, but the gift of the Holy Spirit given by God for building up the body of Christ.

**7. God will not be mocked. We shall all reap whatever we've sown.**

Paul reminds his readers that God cannot be "mocked" – scornfully disregarded – because his judgment is completely just, cf. "since you judge others for doing these things, why do you think you can avoid God's judgment when you do the same things?" (Rom. 2:3, NLT).

**8. If we've sown to the flesh… if we've sown to the Spirit.**

While Paul is speaking in general terms, in one sense "sowing to the flesh" means looking to the flesh for one's benefit and direction, while "sowing to the Spirit" means placing one's confidence and hope in the working of God's Spirit.

According to Hays, v. 8 is not simply a moralistic nod against sensual indulgence, but a warning against placing confidence in anything that belongs to the realm of the "merely human" – particularly circumcision. His point is that only the Spirit of God has the power to confer life.

**9. So let's not grow weary in our well doing.**

Our efforts at "well doing" should not be thought of as autonomous performances on our own part, but as Spirit-empowered manifestations of God at work within us, cf. "it is God who works in you to will and to act in order to fulfill his good purpose" (Phil. 2:13, NIV).

**10. Do good to all people, especially those belonging to the household of faith.**

By "all people," Paul is expanding the sphere of our moral concern to the larger world. By "household of faith," he is reminding us that our membership within the community of God's people depends from first to last on faith – and not membership within the body of ethnic Israel.

**11. Take note of the large letters in this writing, for I am writing them to you with my own hand!**

A common practice in the ancient world was for an amanuensis or scribe to write out the body of a letter by dictation, while the actual sender would write out the final words of the letter in their own writing. The "large letters" mean that Paul has now taken the pen from his scribe and begun composing with his own hand.

For other passages in which Paul personally writes a concluding phrase or paragraph, see 1 Cor. 16:21, Col. 4:18, Philemon 19, 2 Thess. 3:17.

**12-13. So they can avoid persecution... so they can boast in your conversion.**

Paul's argument is that the rival teachers in Galatia were only urging Christian Gentiles to be circumcised to avoid persecution and gain a basis for their boasting. By compelling non-Jewish Christians to be circumcised what they are really doing is asserting the superiority of Jewish religion over non-Jewish expressions of faith in the Messiah.

## 14. May I never boast in anything except for the cross of our Lord Jesus Christ.

To "boast" in the cross – *the place where all human effort and pride come to an end* – is to "boast" in the saving work of Christ and the new reality brought about through his resurrection.

## 15. Neither circumcision nor uncircumcision...but new creation.

What Christ brings through his resurrection is not a new religion or philosophy, but a transformed world, i.e., a new creation! What Paul is here claiming is that the God who created the world has now come to reclaim and transform it. The basis for Paul's hope is none less than Israel's Scriptures, particularly Isaiah 65:17-25, which sets forth a prophetic vision of God's transformative justice.

> See, I will create new heavens and a new earth. The former things will not be remembered, nor will they come to mind. (Isa. 65:17, NIV)

For a non-Jewish believer to be circumcised and follow the Law as a way of being in the right with God was for them to reenter the very world that had been crucified with Christ.

> And from now on we are to call no one by the flesh. And even though we once knew Christ in this way, *we know him by the flesh no longer.* So if anyone is in Christ, then they are a new creation; the old things have passed away; and behold, new things have risen in their place. (2 Cor. 5:16-17)

## 16. Peace and mercy upon all those who walk by this standard.

Paul's blessing is not simply pronounced on all his readers, or the Galatian churches in general, but on those who walk "in alignment" or "in step" (stoicheó) with the measure of truth outlined in v. 15. To do so is to walk by the Spirit (cf. 5:25).

The blessing of "peace and mercy" is deeply traditional and Jewish in character, and corresponds to the Hebrew blessing of *shalom (peace, wholeness)* and *chesed (grace, mercy).*

### The Israel of God.

Paul has already asserted that Gentile believers are children of Abraham, heirs of God's promised blessings (3:6-9, 29; 4:28, 31), and those who fulfill the Law (5:14, 6:2). By "Israel of God," Paul now means all those who are in Christ, whether ethnically Jewish or Gentile, cf. "the household of faith" (6:10).

### 17. I bear in my body the marks of Jesus.

Paul sees the injuries and wounds he has incurred in the course of his apostolic labors as the outward marks of his identification with Christ. By his own testimony he had suffered numerous floggings and beatings for the sake of Jesus and his ministry (2 Cor. 11:23-25, 2 Cor. 6:4-5, Acts 14:19), and the wounds incurred from these beatings were now the mark of his own faith.

## 18. The grace of our Lord Jesus Christ be with your spirit.

For Paul, grace is the basic disposition of God towards creation. It is His willingness to restore what is fallen, save what is lost, and enable what has been weakened through sin.

He ends his short letter just as he began it, by wishing the grace of our Lord Jesus Christ upon his readers.

**Amen.**

# Bibliography

## PRIMARY SOURCES

*The Dead Sea Scrolls in English,* tr. by Vermes, G. (1962)
*Greek NT: Byzantine Majority Text.* Pierpont, W. & Robinson, M. (2005)
*The Greek Testament.* Alford, H. (1884)
*Josephus. Antiquities of the Jews* (AD 93 or 94)
*Josephus. The Jewish War* (circa AD 75)
*The Letter of Aristeas,* ed. Charles, R.H. (1913)
*The Lexham English Septuagint.* Lexham (2019)
*Nestle 1904 Greek New Testament.* Nestle, E. (1904)
*Novum Testamentum Graece.* Ed. by Aland, B., Aland, K., et al (1898)

## COMMENTARIES

Augustine, *Epistle to the Galatians*, n.d.
Betz, H.D., *Galatians: A Commentary on Paul's Letter...* (1979)
Dunn, J. D. G., *The Epistle To The Galatians* (1993)
Hays, R.B., *The Letter to the Galatians. The New Interpreter's Bible, Vol. 11* (2000)
Longenecker, R.N., *Galatians,* WBC 41 (1990)
Martyn, J.L., *Galatians* (1997)
Williams, S.K., *Galatians,* ANTC (1997)
Wright, N.T., *Galatians* in *Commentaries for Christian Formation* (2021)

## OTHER STUDIES

Arminius, J., *Works of James Arminius, Vol. 2, Grace and Free Will* (1560–1609)
Bauckham, R., *God Crucified: Monotheism and Christology in the NT* (1998)
Bauckham, R., *Paul's Christology of Divine Identity* (2016)

Duffield, G. & Van Cleave, N. M., *Foundations of Pentecostal Theology* (1983)

Gaventa, B. R., *The Maternity of Paul: An Exegetical Study of Galatians* (1990)

Hayford, J., *Hayford's Bible Handbook* (1995)

Hays, R. B., *The Conversion of the Imagination: Paul as Interpreter of...* (2005)

Hays, R. B., *Echoes of Scripture in the Letters of Paul* (1993)

Heiser, M.S., *The Unseen Realm: Recovering the Supernatural Worldview* (2015)

Hengel, M., *The Zealots: Investigations into the Jewish Freedom Movement* (1961)

Menzies, W. & Horton, S. M., *Bible Doctrines: A Pentecostal Perspective* (1993)

Sanders, E.P., *Paul and Palestinian Judaism* (1977)

Simon, M., *Romans: The Gospel of Grace* (2023)

Von Rad, G., *Old Testament Theology I* (1962)

Wright, N.T. & Bird, M.F., *The New Testament in Its World* (2019)

# Meet the Author

MARC D. SIMON is an ordained minister with the International Church of the Foursquare Gospel and serves as the senior teaching pastor of Church For The Nations, in Oxnard, CA. Marc holds graduate degrees in Psychology, Organizational Leadership, and Theology, and also serves as a chaplain with the Ventura County Rescue Mission.

Printed in the United States
by Baker & Taylor Publisher Services